NOTES FROM A FAILURE

*Stories That Might Make You Laugh, Feel Sorry For Me,
or Teach You Amazing Life Lessons*

written by
Daniel CJ Grant

Grant, Daniel CJ.
    NOTES FROM A FAILURE - Stories That Might Make You Laugh, Feel Sorry For Me, or Teach You Amazing Life Lessons / Daniel CJ Grant
        ISBN 978-0-9919299-4-8

1

FOREWORD

I've never been a success financially. That automatically puts me in the failure category for most people.

I had a good run with baseball, both as a player and a coach, but I don't know if "wildly successful" can be said in the post-career summary.

I was never the most popular kid.

I ran a "successful" business for a couple years but it died.

I've found and married the perfect woman but, man, did it take going through thick, gross mud to get to her (and even when she appeared I almost missed it).

I've piled up debt with bad choices and pipe dreams.

I wrote a book and so far it pays for my Netflix subscription.

I had easy opportunities but I was too scared to take them.

I followed too much and let others control my life.

I've always been scared to death to speak my mind.

That book I mentioned a few sentences ago was about my battles with severe depression and anxiety. So for a bulk of my life I dealt with those joys.

But — I know this is hard to believe — I didn't write this book for you to feel bad for me. I wrote it for your entertainment and my sanity to a degree. I've always found it helps talking about my failures and embarrassments. After a while they all become kind of fun to tell. And I like making people laugh, so hopefully you'll laugh a little reading. Some stories aren't funny but who cares?

If you find lessons in my failures then that's a bonus…a huge bonus. A bonus I would sincerely love to be a result of these stories.

I'm sweating writing this foreword because I'm scared. Scared of what you'll think of me. Scared you'll make fun of me for saying no to the hot cheerleader who wanted to trade pants. Scared you'll hate me drinking so much while on scholarship to play a game I loved. Scared you'll think I'm a loser for not holding my business together.

For most of my life I've been a gigantic failure.

I have plenty more embarrassing stories and tales of failure but these will do for now. Plus, there are more in my "hot-selling" book, *The War On Self.*

On the outside everything looked happy and amazing; in reality, it was a disaster.

Yes, I'm scared. But that's the only way I share a piece of my work now. If I'm scared to do it.

So here it is.

There are serious, meaningful, funny, sad, and touching stories in this little collection.

I have to say James Altucher was a big inspiration for this series of stories. His vulnerable honesty seemed to give me a green-light to share my issues and failings. If you haven't read his stuff, do it.

I hope you get something out of it and I hope I start finding most of these stories funnier and funnier to tell.

Thank you for reading and, truthfully, I hope you find the humor in most of these stories.

Daniel CJ Grant (while sweating profusely at the thought of other people reading this)
    danielcjgrant@gmail.com

2

HOURS AND HOURS ON THE PHONE

We were both in relationships we were tired of. We each wanted better but were scared to get out. Some nights we talked for hours, giving each other advice and hope.

I would be in Alberta, my sister in Ontario. It sucked knowing better was out there but not having the gusto to take that shot in finding it. Like sucked really bad. Sleepless nights, boring phone conversations (with my girlfriend, not my sister), nightly email updates on what I did that day. You see my girlfriend was in school in America. Probably a good thing now because if she wasn't I'd be married to her with three kids. That's how little balls I had.

I eventually did make the move. We broke up over the phone and she told me to call her when I got back from a conference in Louisville. I never did. I never spoke to her again. There were only two emails sent after the breakup. You have to disappear. Why let it linger?

I texted my sister telling her the news. She called, I broke down, she talked me back up, I broke down some more. I knew it was for the best but I was extremely upset at how my girlfriend took our split. Awful.

I can't stand breaking a heart. But it was all okay. Plus going to Louisville so soon after helped immensely. While there I paid the piano guy at the bar $10 to play, *O Canada*. I stood with my hand over my heart as 300 people booed wildly. Then some guy came up and paid $20 to get him to stop immediately and play, *The Star Spangled Banner*.

It is incredible how you can bring so much emotion out of people for $10.

Today I'm married and it's to a woman who I'm excited to see every single day. We truly love talking with each other and pondering what's in each other's brain.

In a couple weeks my sister is getting married. I'm happy to say it's not with the guy we had long conversations about. He's a great guy and I'm happy for them both.

My sister and I haven't had any long conversations about relationships in forever. Ever since we started seeing our new gems in fact.

I guess sometimes you have to go through hundreds of long, frustrating phone calls before you don't have to do it anymore.

3

HOW I KILLED MY BUSINESS IN LESS THAN TWO

YEARS

It all started a little too easy. I put one ad in the newspaper and before the first day of bootcamp I had over 30 people signed up. By that October, after a promotion with a soccer team, I had over 60 squeezed so tightly in the room I rented I had to stand in one spot the entire workout. It was a fire hazard plus some.

Then I started getting tired and bored. Not necessarily with the people, but the business.

This happens to me a lot. I get bored fast. One month it can be the most interesting thing in the world and the next it feels like that old joke your grandpa has told you a thousand times. You still chuckle, out of respect, but it's worn out its welcome.

When I shut down my business to get back into coaching baseball I had 6 people in the bootcamp and, I think, 18 private clients.

The bootcamp portion of my business paid the price. I let too much drama get involved. One night I received a call ten minutes before the bootcamp was starting from a girl I paid to run it. She was crying, calling to find out if the rumors were true if I'd kissed a certain girl. I was single and twenty-eight years old. Of course I'm kissing girls who want me to kiss them.

One member started crying one workout because she told me her shoulder injury might be "all in her head." I said, "It might be."

Apparently, you should never agree with a female that her problems are probably psychological.

People lost weight and some drastically altered their life for the better. And it was awesome. But I lost interest in the business.

One time, a member brought four puppies to bootcamp. With only four people showing up we decided to take the puppies for a walk and not workout.

I fell out of love with training. Coming up with workouts was becoming overly consuming and stressful. I took program design seriously and would debate for hours if I had enough pull exercises compared to push exercises. Whether a certain exercise would benefit. All of it was tiring and I started to hate it.

I had business coaches I was paying four hundred dollars a month for one fifteen minute conversation on the phone.

Upsell this, upsell that, get emails, create online products. It's all about squeezing every dime you can get out of a person and making money while you sleep. It was fucking exhausting listening to this bullshit. But I bought in and believed it was what I had to do.

I started selling supplements. I wrote programs and gave special offers to my members. Since nobody else would buy them it wasn't really a special offer. It was the only offer.

So I allowed learned helplessness to enter my business and I gave up trying to grow it anymore.

When a baseball coaching opportunity came to me it was perfect, because now I had a reason to shut the business down.

4

THE SLAP SHOT THAT CHANGED THE WORLD

"Just don't break the window."

Those were the famous words spoken by my mother as her and my father left for a walk.

On my very next slap shot, with them only half a block away, I shattered our front window.

I forget how old I was. Mid-teens I would guess. I was never good at the slap shot. Whether I was on skates or in shoes in my driveway, I sucked at it. My wrist shot was pretty good. My stick handling was average at best. But my slap shot? It was worse than the taste of ketchup on cornflakes.

That night, however, it was amazing. And by amazing I mean amazing. I could place it anywhere in the net. I was even calling post shots. I was in a zone. A zone that was mystical to me.

I started imagining scenarios where the game was on the line and it was only my slap shot hitting the inside left post and deflecting in that would win the game. And I did it.

When my parents came out of the house I had already been pounding shots for half an hour. I even showed them my incredible accuracy.

They looked nervous.

Then they walked past me to begin their walk.

Then I placed my next slap shot through the window. And I wasn't aiming for the window.

I ran into the house, saw glass everywhere on the kitchen floor, looked at our dog hiding under a table in the living room, and continued the run to my room.

After wild screaming, crying, and a new window, the slap shot was outlawed forever in our driveway, and a "tennis ball only" rule now in place. I never took a slap shot again. At least not the kind of slap shots I was talking that fateful night.

I lost it forever. That one shinning moment only I got to be a part of it. I was the only person in the world to see those amazing slap shots. I was the only one to see the window busting shot too. Everyone else just heard it.

I was sad I broke the window. It cost my parents a good amount of money. But I'm mainly sad that I gave up the slap shot. That I let new rules stop my momentum.

Who knows, maybe I could have been one of the greatest driveway slap shot shooters the world had ever seen.

I don't know. No one will ever know.

5

WHY THERE IS ALWAYS A CHANCE I SHOW UP TO A

PARTY IN SWEATPANTS

It was my first semester at the University of Northern Iowa. I was having a great time for the most part. I was dealing with some separation anxiety because my girlfriend still lived in Canada. On my last night in Thunder Bay before I left for school we decided we should go out.

Never make that decision.

My personality as a carefree human evolved rapidly one night as I became exhausted trying to look good and impress people. So I went out wearing sweatpants and an old t-shirt. I didn't even comb my hair. I looked like I had literally just gotten out of bed.

It was a Saturday night, which meant it was a party night. There was a get together at a few of my teammates house.

After some pre-drinks at my apartment it was time to head out. Our first stop was a bar on campus. Everyone got carded but me. Something about looking near homeless gets you mini-benefits I guess.

We hit the dance floor and every teammate I saw made comments about my dress code for the evening. They mainly thought it was hilarious.

After an hour or so we decided it was finally time to jet to the party. It was the typical party scene. Everybody in their nicer clothes. All the guys doing everything in their power to be close to girls. Most of the girls huddling together as a form of protection from the vultures.

When I walked in I got the same reaction from the guys as I did at the bar.

I started to think I was on to something. They made it sound like I was the first human being to ever go to a college party in sweatpants. Apparently different draws more attention because this was the first time I was this popular right out of the gates.

As the night progressed I found myself talking to one of my friends in the kitchen. He left to go play video games I think, so I was left alone.

I didn't care. It was my carefree night.

Soon a small, very good-looking girl came and sat on the counter next to me. She introduced herself and said she was a cheerleader. I introduced myself and said I was a baseball player.

She asked where I was from. I said, Canada. She was from Iowa. Girls don't usually approach me at parties so this was weird for me at first.

She mentioned how the party was getting a little boring and I agreed.

Then she started telling me how she had never "been" with a Canadian before. She had always wanted to. She had heard Canadians are "good in bed and have big cocks." And she liked both of those things.

I agreed emphatically.

She shuffled herself over and was now touching the side of my arm with her leg. She looked at me and said, "I'm so jealous of your outfit, you look so comfortable."

"I am," I said.

"God, I wish I was in sweatpants. These jeans are so uncomfortable."

"Well, they do look pretty tight," I said.

She laughed. "Did you want to trade," she continued, her mouth forming a grin.

"What do you mean?"

"I want to wear your sweatpants. Let's get out of here and I'll trade you pants."

I mumbled something about her pants not fitting around my ankles and she assured me that was the point.

But, instead of having the easiest sex I could ever get with a gorgeous female, I turned it down. In an amazingly awkward way too, I should add.

I had a girlfriend I'd only gone out on one date with. It wasn't actually even a date. It was a work get together to celebrate the end of summer and we ended up at a park alone and had our "talk." If we never had that alone time I would have been sharing my sweatpants and discovering what the cheerleaders point was.

6

THANK YOU ALCOHOLISM!

When I woke up in Evansville, IN, I knew I had taken it too far. My need for alcohol, that is. From wrecking my hamstring permanently to being put on Prozac, there was a large spiral of downward falling in my life. So I partied to make all my problems go away.

Well, that's only half true. I partied 3 to 4 times a week. I drank 7. When I got back to my apartment after the days schooling or practice I reached into my closet to grab the bottle of Canadian Club Whiskey and the bottle of Ginger Ale. I had at least two or three a night, and they weren't in small quantities.

I started doing strange things that were rare for me. Partying until 5am, getting woken up at 7am to be driven home so I could change, and then going to school for an 8am test I didn't study for. Going to karaoke night every Wednesday, drinking mass amounts of beer and singing, *Your Body Is*

A Wonderland; or going up as a group and me screaming into the mic, "U-N-I BASEBALL BITCHES!!!" during every pause in our song of choice.

The night I tore my hamstring we were in Kentucky, 45 minutes outside of Nashville. One of the parents snuck a few of us out and we went to Music City. Curfew was at midnight so we had four hours. We drank on the way down and had the time of our lives for the two and a half hours we were there. I made it back to my room at 11:58pm.

The weird thing about that night was my watch. When we entered the city limits I looked down to see what time it was. I saw the second hand move and then stop. My watch just stopped working. The entire night it was the same time. As we left Nashville I happened to peak down and it began ticking again. By far, the eeriest thing I've ever experienced. Except for that time I thought a ghost was taking a piss in the corner of my hotel room.

The twenty-four hour period that shifted me away from booze started on the last day of exams. As a team, we all went to celebrate at a bar near my apartment. As I was commencing to down my first drink I made a public announcement I was going to down twenty-four drinks that night. My roommate would keep track. After the twelfth drink I started lying and counted each drink as two. Wandering around a bar and spending time on the dance floor made it easy to loose track of me. So I didn't reach twenty-four, but I drank too much, that was clear.

We were traveling to Indiana the next morning for a weekend series and our coach decided -- most likely trying to avoid us partying so much the night before -- to have practice at 8am before the bus left.

I got home at 3am with my Japanese teammate who made us some Ramen Noodles with soy sauce and a raw egg. It was delicious. And then I passed out.

At 7:30am I was woken up and we drove to practice. Still drunk, I warmed up and went to the cages to hit. I had the best round in months since my disastrous injury. I couldn't feel any pain in my leg. When I stepped out of the cage my coach came up to me and said, "Whatever you're doing, keep doing it. That's the best your swing's been since your hamstring went."

I said, "Yes, sir," praying he wouldn't smell me, and kind of chuckling at the same time.

Practice, somehow, went without a hitch. I actually felt pretty awesome.

My roommates and I stopped at Burger King before we went to pick up our travel gear and that's when it hit me. Standing in line to order, my world started spinning like a tornado. I felt nauseous and dizzy. I stumbled back to the car and closed my eyes. When we got to the apartment I walked in my room and collapsed on my bed.

I hadn't packed for the trip yet and my room was a mess, so when I was woken up from my coma I threw anything I could find into my travel bag. I just hoped I remembered my jock strap and a toothbrush. There is nothing worse than forgetting your toothbrush.

We got to the bus, I went to my seat, sat down and passed out.

Nine hours later I awoke in Evansville.

I missed dinner. The team said I was feeling sick and needed rest so they left me in the bus.

I felt amazing when I woke up, but the message was clear. I was fucking my life up in a big way.

That night I didn't swear off drinking but I swore off getting drunk for a while. I also started taking myself off my pills. I needed control of my life back.

I've found addiction to anything is bad. Drinking isn't bad. Too much drinking is bad.

Alcohol taught me a great lesson in that way.

7

THE NIGHT I DROVE MY CAR THROUGH THE

CHURCH'S FENCE

"Grandpa, I need to tell you something. I just crashed my car through your fence."

This was, by far, the most embarrassing moment of my life up to that point. Even more so than the time I was helping with communion and was attacked by sloppy kisses from a young girl in the crowd. I was like 4 or 5. She was like 3 or 4. Although I don't really remember it, I'm sure it was highly embarrassing.

My grandpa, to his credit, stayed calm and followed me outside to see the damage.

After seeing the crushed front end of the old Volvo I was driving — it was my other grandpa's car at one time and he sold it to my dad a year earlier — and the giant hole in the fence, my grandpa said, "I'll drive you home after and we will tell your folks then."

As devastated as I was, I felt a certain peace from his calming nature.

I was there, at the church, with my friend. My grandpa was the Pastor and was holding an adult meeting informing people on what church is for those curious. My friend was curious, so I told him I would take him.

That night my buddy came by the house a few minutes before we were supposed to leave. My parents were out at dinner and I don't know where my siblings were. My brother was probably out eating seagull eggs (a story for another time, maybe).

Anyways, it was dark out and it was the first time I ever drove at night. Ever.

We got in the car and, as I started the car, my WWF (now WWE) cassette tape blasted a professional wrestlers theme song. But the lights in the car didn't turn on. I clicked some buttons but nothing happened. My friend tried a couple things. Nothing worked.

I wondered if I should drive with the lights not on. It was pitch black in the vehicle and I could barely see the shift stick. The drive to the church was only five minutes so we didn't think it was that big of deal. So we went.

Along the way a few cars flashed their headlights at me but, overall, it was very uneventful.

Until we entered the parking lot.

With Mark Henry's theme song, *Sexual Chocolate*, blaring through the speakers, I began turning into a parking spot by the grandparent's house (which was right next to the church). For whatever reason, instead of moving my foot to hit the breaks, which I thought I was doing, I punched the gas and accelerated through the fence.

My friend later told me he thought he heard me say, "watch this," as I started turning towards the parking spot. I don't remember anything. I know I wanted to park the car so I don't know why I would say that and then bang into a fence with it.

I sat, silent, as the roundtable discussion about God and church happened around me. There was no doubt in my mind I would be murdered by my parents when I got home.

As the night went a question was raised, "who is God to you?"

Everybody gave some sort of generic answer to the question.

"He is my Savior."

"God is my guide."

I don't know. It all sounded like bullshit to me.

When it was my turn I said, "I guess God, whatever you believe, is an opportunity to do good in whatever situation you are in. If you're rich you can help the poor. If you're homeless and you are given a sandwich to eat you can give half to the homeless guy next to you. Everybody can do good; it's just a choice. Your belief is an opportunity to how you act."

It was my favorite thing I said during my teenage years. Maybe it wasn't, I don't know. I was proud I didn't say something generic and predictable in one short sentence.

As the talk finished the knot — already in my gut — tightened even more. I was scared to death.

After dropping my friend off at his house it was time to go home and tell my parents why grandpa was dropping me off.

I walked in the door and sat down at the kitchen table, and started sobbing.

My grandpa told the story, left, and I got yelled at, and I think grounded. I can't remember. I was happy enough not to be taken out to the back and shot.

I went to my room thinking I never wanted to drive at night, ever again.

8

THE ONLY NIGHT I'VE EVER HAD GAME AND

CRACKING OPEN MY FRIENDS SKULL

As a college kid, Panama City during Spring Break is a pretty awesome place to be. I was there playing baseball, but we were allowed one free day.

The night before the free day many of us would get into Club La Vela and pay one of our teammates older brother to buy us shots. We would do our best to hide near a staircase and ram as many tequila shots down as we could before we were either broke or trashed.

After the bar — we still had a curfew — we walked out and I saw a Lipton Iced Tea booth. I said I wanted a t-shirt (the amount of free shit you can get at Spring Break is ridiculous). The girls in the booth said that if I wanted a t-shirt I would have to grab a girl from the bar entrance line and get her to kiss me.

Being drunk this didn't seem hard.

I walked over and found the prettiest girl in the line. I went up to her and told her I needed her "for a second." She surprisingly left her group without hesitation.

"Okay, now tell her your best pickup line and if she will kiss you after you get a shirt."

Boy, did I want this shirt. But pickup lines were never my strong suit.

I leaned in and whispered, "I never believed in heaven until I saw you." Probably the cheesiest thing you can say, ever, to a girl.

She repeated what I said to the girls behind the booth and they "awed," which surprised me even more.

So we kissed. A little peck. That wasn't good enough for the t-shirt though. They wanted a show. So we made out. It was pretty awesome making out with a hot girl for a t-shirt. It's been the only time in my life I have ever had game. To make it clear how little game I have, it took me over a month to figure my future wife was hitting on me before we started dating.

I got my t-shirt and left. Never saw that girl again or made any further moves. Wait, maybe I didn't have game? Why would I just leave? The t-shirt was a good enough capper to the evening, I guess.

The next morning a few of us decided to rent scooters and drive around the city. The rental place was a thirty-second walk from our hotel.

We took 10 minutes to learn the basics and get comfortable.

Then, it was time to go.

I went first and all my training knowledge disappeared.

I punched the gas a little too fast and flew onto a busy street and was inches away from being destroyed by a huge black truck.

My mind went into hyper focus as I narrowly avoided death and I hooked a right on a grassy area next to the road, still cruising at top speed. I was quickly coming to another street so I had two options: jump onto the busy road ahead or hook a left before it.

I hooked a left and ended up in a big ditch going as fast as this thing could go. As I was driving in this uneven, bumpy ditch I was just trying to stay upright.

After the few seconds — which felt like eternity — of my time in the ditch my mind clicked back into thinking mode and reminding me to take my hand of the gas. If I wanted to slow down and not die, that is.

I did want to slow down. And I can assure you I didn't want to die.

I remembered how to use the break and I stopped, in the middle of a ditch next to a bunch of drunk kids yelling how awesome that was. I'm happy they enjoyed it.

A minute later by buddies finally caught up to me.

"What the hell was that?"

"I don't know. I forgot how to stop."

The rest of the afternoon was peaceful and enjoyable, now that I knew how to stop and slow down.

The next morning I found myself in one of those blowup boxing rings you wear big gloves and fight. My roommate wanted to fight me. He was stronger than I was but the cushion in the gloves made it extremely safe to punch each other.

We went in, got geared up, and went after it. We flailed at each other and I was pushed down a couple times.

Then, out of nowhere, I got a nice shot in and he stumbled back. I took advantage and sent a punishing haymaker his way. Unfortunately as that punch was heading toward his skull the bar you hold onto in the glove came loose. The bar stabbed him near the top of his forehead. He went down fast. I went down with him. It's very unstable on a blown up boxing ring.

I looked up and saw nothing but blood. The entire half of the ring was a red sea.

I glanced at my glove and noticed the bar sticking out of the glove. Oh shit, I thought, I just killed our catcher.

The blood flooded his face. I took my t-shirt off and gave it to him to press on the wound. It was my Lipton Iced Tea shirt.

We caused Panama City to shut the boxing ring down that year. We were the last to fight. And I won. I can't say I didn't feel a tiny bit good about it. I was the tough guy who closed down an entire game.

I did feel bad for my friend. It was his birthday and he had to spend most of it getting stitches in his skull.

Good thing I was wearing my Lipton Iced Tea shirt. I wouldn't have given him one of my regular shirts.

9

MY DRUNK $3000 BUSINESS DECISION

I was drunk. I had already talked to who would be my mentors about the opportunity. It sounded good. Really good.

I would only have to invest $1500 upfront and then pay a minimal fee every month (ie. buy the product). Ten people were all I really needed to sign up before I started making money. Big money. You know, that luxurious type of money where I go skiing in Colorado and party with models in Paris while money pours into my bank account.

I first found out about it from a well-known self-help guy. I was really into reading his stuff and when he came out and spewed his bullshit on how he thought he would never get into multi-level marketing again but this company was just "too amazing," I bought in.

What a fucking idiot I was.

Gullible and looking for a better life was my current situation so it all sounded good.

So I wanted more information. I got a call from a couple people telling me how simple it was and how amazing the product was.

The company sold multivitamins in a gel form pretty much. The stuff tasted good too.

Anyways, back to the "I was drunk" part.

I was at a party with some friends and I snuck away to check my email. One of my friends walked by and asked why the hell I was checking email during a party. I started talking about this business.

"It's only $1500 to get in and I should be able to make that back relatively easy. I'm thinking I should just do it. I want to be a business owner."

"Yeah, it sounds good."

Another friend joined in, "That does sound good. If it works out, I'll join."

Being an idiot, I assumed I already had my first member because why wouldn't this work out?

So, while I was drunk and full of hope I whipped out my credit card and gave them all my information.

I was officially a business owner.

I was also officially a moron.

The next week a huge box of product arrived. I worked as a rehab therapist at a chiropractor's office at the time, so I thought this should be an easy sell to clients.

Who wouldn't want to suck down their vitamins in thick, gooey, heavenly fashion?

Almost everybody it turned out.

I would stay up late listening to my self-help teach me how to set up meetings where people come over to my house — or a place I rented, preferably — and I sold them on this body altering gel. And to become a part of this amazing product line they would only have to give me $1500.

I sent a thousand emails to anybody in a health profession, telling them about this once in a lifetime opportunity.

Every month, more and more product would show up at my door, and more money would be charged to my credit card.

After about eight months and zero new members I was exhausted.

I'm not the greatest salesman, which played a huge part. I should have heavily thought about that before I chose to go into a business that required me doing desperate amounts of it.

Luckily I somehow found somebody in the city to buy the remaining product off of me for about $400. It was at least $800 worth of shit.

Buying in to fluffy promises was a mistake. It's always a mistake. My first harsh lesson dealing with top-level salespeople. The drunk part wasn't so bright either.

Actually I would say you should never make any decision drunk other then going to bed and maybe taking an aspirin.

It could save you over $3000.

10

THE TRUTH RIGHT NOW

My brain has a hard time letting me say what I want to say. I'm scared of the feedback. What if I'm wrong? What if people hate me? What if they make fun of me? It's just way too overwhelming to deal with.

I've always been scared of failure. Growing up, playing baseball I was almost always the best on the field. I didn't personally feel that way, but it was true.

My dad liked answering questions people asked me about baseball. They would ask how it was going and my dad would tell them all the great things I did last game. I felt embarrassed by it for some reason. I started believing nobody found what I had to say interesting.

I still struggle with that belief.

My self-confidence has always been a little fragile. My face turns red thinking about all the moments I wanted to run and hide in a cave. Like the time I was blamed for farting in my fourth grade class when it clearly wasn't me. Or the time my teacher yelled at me for taking so long to put my glasses on and come to her desk to read something for her. I hated wearing glasses. Or the time I met a girl at a party, hit it off, invited her to hangout in the baseball player section of the school, and when she came I got embarrassed, turned red, and could barely speak. Oh, and the time I told people in a meeting my idea and they all laughed at me, so I stopped telling people my ideas.

I have found it to be strange gaining a minuscule army of people following my writing and enjoying it. The more people who tell me they love my stuff the more people I have to avoid starting to hate me. So sometimes I don't say everything I want to say because I might upset them.

It makes writing incredibly difficult.

Maybe if I just put some thoughts in bullet points then you can decide whether you love me, like me, or hate me. Then we can all move on and I won't have to worry about what you think of me all the time.

• The true problem with professional sports is the fans. We supply the money so they can live luxurious lifestyles playing games. Stop blaming the athletes. If you were that good you wouldn't mind getting paid handsomely for it.

• Most people are stupid. Not because they are dumb, but because they've bought into this society of staring at screens, keeping track with celebrities, and suffering in jobs that are killing them. There are more reasons and, don't worry, I'm stupid too. I have wasted my fair share of time on all that crap.

• If I were to do it over again — and didn't play baseball — I wouldn't have gone to college. I would have started a business at 18, failed, then started another. By 22 I would have been further ahead of graduates trying to find the job I had at 18. My degree has only helped me get one job and it sucked.

•   I don't know why people call me pessimistic. It's how you create great comedy.

•   I don't get why people need more and more money. But, at the same time, I'd love all that money and would live on an island and forget about all the real problems in the world.

•   That above point isn't totally true. I love helping charity and want to create my own scholarship fund where I give someone $80,000 to create art for one year and showcase it at the end of that year. Maybe then they can live their passion.

•   The Office (US Version) and Curb Your Enthusiasm are the two greatest television shows in history. Three's Company, The George Burns and Gracie Allen Show, and Cheers are runner-ups.

•   There is too much noise and flashing lights at concerts now. We need to bring back a man and his guitar in a smoky theatre.

•   I constantly wonder why we all care so much what others think. Pretty odd statement considering the subject of this article, isn't it?

•   I used to love going to movies. Now I don't. Most of them are shit. Actually, they were mostly shit when I loved going. It just took me awhile to figure it out.

•   I hate horror movies but I feel I'd be a really good horror writer.

•   I just realized how ridiculous this article is. Maybe because my brain is furious at me for sharing random opinions I, for some reason, want to share.

11

MY PERSONAL GROUNDHOG DAY FROM MENTAL

HELL

I blew it. Threw the game away. Easy ground ball, easy throw, and I botched it. I threw a sinker to the first baseman, the ball skipped by him, they scored, we lost. Thank goodness they had to beat us twice to win the Provincial Championship.

We won the second game, so we ended up leaving that day as Provincial Champs, but if we'd lost that game I would have cried far more than I did after blowing game one for us. Being 17 and carrying the world on your shoulders sucks. Especially when you're the only one putting that kind of pressure on yourself.

The horrible throw I made that afternoon haunted me. I never wanted to play shortstop again.

The next summer we played an exhibition game against the team we beat in the finals. We were at a different stadium, however.

In the ninth, the exact same situation from the finals happened. Same count, same score, same ground ball, same throw, same result.

As soon as I let the ball out of my hand I knew we lost. It didn't help during the entire ninth inning I was obsessed about how this Groundhog Day situation was materializing. Things were going perfectly the same as they did eight months earlier.

Same leadoff single. Same passed ball. Same strikeout. Same stolen base. It was all *too* eerily the same. I didn't want that ground ball hit to me. I knew what would happen.

I wouldn't lob it to the second baseman to get the force out because I thought there wasn't enough time. I would field it clean but get a bad grip on the ball and, instead of taking a split second to fix it, I would rush the throw. The ball would dive, hit a divot in the dirt, and skip by our lunging first baseman.

And that's what happened.

It's easy to say you can't let your problems linger. But that second throw turned me into a mental midget for a while. I didn't want any ground ball hit to me.

But if you live through that fear long enough, and don't run away, the answers can start to appear. It was that second brutal throw that got me interested in the mental side of life. Sure, for years after all of this I still had a lot of depression and anxiety issues in my life. But from a baseball perspective I did alright.

Two years after that Groundhog Day error I was holding a Junior College World Series Championship trophy. I played shortstop that year. The last season I ever played shortstop, in fact.

It's strange how some failures can brand your brain with hot metal scarring you forever, and some you can get past fairly well.

Most of it must have to do with your comfort towards the activity you've failed at. I took baseball seriously and any type of failure killed me.

Luckily, thanks to natural ability and passion I seemed to always bounce back pretty quick. If I failed with females I would be devastated and question my stature as a man. Same with business. Failing at business made me feel weak and humiliated.

Maybe it's attitude. Maybe some things you just can't overcome. I know that's "negative" and not what you're supposed to tell people in this sensitive world, but maybe it's true. Maybe it's okay to fail and give up. Maybe it's not. I don't know.

That's the beauty of this whole life. None of us really know.

12

I, APPARENTLY, DON'T LIKE EASY SEX

"Just take one for the team," this guy, I just met that night, told me. He was a friend of the girl who was obsessed with me. We were at her going away party and the only reason I was there was because all my workmates wanted me to go.

"She really likes you and it's only one time," he continued. You know when someone is telling you these kind of things the girl is not attractive.

I replied, "I don't think so."

But that didn't stop the sales pitch.

It all started while I was drunk at a bar. I went out with my friends from work. She happened to be there. My work consisted of two separate groups: my group of four people and the other group of 30. We never saw each other except for Monday mornings when we would all gather for a big meeting. That's all you really need to know.

At the bar that night she came up and started talking to me. I was drunk and very enthusiastic about all things life at that moment (you know, that kind of drunk). She asked me a question and I ripped a promotional poster off the wall and wrote my number on it. I don't remember why she needed my number. But I was enthusiastic and more then willing. This was entirely my fault.

The next morning the phone rang. I mumbled a greeting and heard her voice. How did she get my number? was my first thought. She wanted to hangout later. I was "busy."

When I arrived for our meeting Monday morning she had saved a seat for me. What the hell was happening?

The next couple weeks turned out the same. She was always lingering around me and saving me seats. How she always knew where I was I will never know.

A week before the going away party one of my female coworkers asked me how Tina (not her real name) was doing?

"Why would you ask me that question?" was my response.

"I thought you two were going out?"

I almost threw up on the spot. Tina had been telling people we were an item for weeks. I didn't know what to do so I did what I usually do: *avoid.*

I definitely didn't want to go to this party now. I had a crush on another girl at work and was baffled when one day she seemed less interested. Well, now I knew why.

The girl I wanted to go out with told me I should come to the party. She now understood I was not going out with Tina so, of course, I wanted to go and hangout with the girl I actually liked.

I met some of Tina's guy friends and all of their first responses were, "so you're the guy." Holy shit!

After an hour I needed to get out. I gathered my workmates (in the group of four) and told them we should make a run for it. They all agreed and we tried sneaking out. It didn't work. Tina saw me leaving. I said we were going to a bar and started walking at a pace many elite speed walkers would have been impressed by.

At the bar I found some more friends and it was shaping up to be a fun night. Then, while talking to a few friends, I felt a hand slip into mine. I knew whose hand it was. I turned my body ever so slightly hoping my friends weren't seeing what was happening.

"I have to take a leak," I said, freeing my hand and giving my friend across from me very distinct directions with my eyes.

I walked to the restroom and, luckily, my friend got the message and followed me.

"I have to get out of here," I said. "That girl is crazy. Stand outside the door and let me know when she is gone."

When he told me she wasn't standing outside the restroom anymore I moved quickly through the maze of people, finding myself outside.

A few of my friends, who happened to be outside, saw me. I told them I was leaving as fast as possible, with no explanation.

I was halfway down the block when I heard, "DAN...DAN...WAIT UP..."

It was Tina.

I stopped and told her I was sorry but I had to go.

"I'll walk with you. My place is on the way to yours. You can stop in for a drink if you want."

"I think I'm just going to find a taxi. It's a long walk."

"It's a great night for a walk, though."

"I'm going to grab a taxi."

We reached a corner store where I stopped to buy a water. She wouldn't leave my side. When I walked back outside I saw a taxi fly by and I started screaming at it, waving my arms wildly. It heard me.

I got in and asked if she wanted to be dropped off at her place.

"No, let's walk," she said.

"No, I'm taking this taxi home."

She started crying. I turned volatile.

"LAST CHANCE. GET IN THE TAXI. I'M LEAVING IN THIS

THING EITHER WAY."

As she sobbed and refused I shut the door and told the taxi to get the fuck out of there.

Looking back, I realize how kind it was of me to leave a female alone, stranded in a shady corner store parking lot, but it wasn't my fault...I'm pleading with you to believe me.

My dad was watching television when I arrived home. He asked me how my night was and I said it was, "fine." Then I saw a folder full of articles. They were Tina's. She had given them to me a week before for some reason. I politely took them and promised to return them before she left.

I ran into the living room and asked my dad if he could drive me to drop these articles off. We had to do it FAST! I told him.

He was confused, but to his credit we got in that car and we started driving, no questions asked.

We stopped in front of Tina's house and I sprinted to her front door and threw them down at her door. I jumped back into the car and with my best, I just dropped a bomb off at that door voice, I said, "move, move, move."

Just as we started moving I saw a figure down the road. I slipped down as low as I could. It was Tina. She was carrying her high heels and crying. It was a sad sight.

Me, peering through the car window, doing my best secret spy impression might have been the saddest sight of all, however.

~~~~~~~~~

I just came off the best year of my life. I had a blast at school and we won the Junior College World Series. I won a ton of awards, including 1st Team All-American and World Series M.V.P. The local news in Thunder Bay even did a five-minute feature report on me when I returned home for the summer.

I was kicking around the men's summer league to stay in baseball mode for the summer before I headed to play Division I baseball at the University of Northern Iowa. After games most of us would head for beers.

She was a waitress at the bar we drank at. She was cute and my cousin didn't hesitate trying to set us up. He also that summer didn't hesitate to convince the DJ at a strip club to call me on stage so three naked strippers could strip me down to my underwear, pour a tub full of oil over all of us, and climb and grind on me. Ah, such a kind fellow, my cousin.

She was nice, but as I drove home that night I thought nothing of it. I assumed she was being nice since it was her job to be so.

A few nights later my mom came downstairs and told me some girl was at the door for me. Yep, you guessed it, it was her. I have no idea how she found out where I lived.

She was sweating. She was out for a jog, she said, and thought she would stop in to say hi. She lived about a fifteen-minute walk away from me. Great.

We sat on the front steps and talked. I forget about what. I was young enough, I guess, I thought it was cool a girl had hunted me down to hangout. So we talked and I told her my plans on going out Saturday night.

The bar was busy and loud; two things I hate. But when you're 19 it can be tolerable. It was $2 MGD and Corona night. We drank a lot of gross, cheap beer, and fast. As I was on the dance floor Krista (not her real name) came up to say hi. We went to grab a drink and talk.

Then it was time to dance. And we danced. Too much dancing. The reason I say that is because after a few songs she came in for a kiss and as I put my hand on her back it was drenched in sweat. Like, not drenched, but like there was a waterfall of warm water flowing down her back. I was too polite to remove my hand.

It was a fun enough night but I went back with my buddies and called it a night. Krista came to another bar night. She wanted me to come back to her place, and most guys would have, but I wasn't into it.

It pissed her off but I told her a momma's boy excuse that I had to be home soon and had a really early morning anyways.

Krista came knocking a few nights later. She wanted to go out. I didn't. She almost too blatantly said she wanted me. I, for some reason that all men would probably condemn me for, didn't. I told her I was going out with a friend already so I couldn't hangout, and hinted never hanging out again.

She stormed off down the pitch black street. I called my friend, pleading with him to come over immediately to go out, just incase Krista came back to the house.

He came over, and as we drove to another friends house we happened to pass by Krista's house. And there she was, in the dark of the night, sitting on the steps of her place, her head in her knees, sobbing.

I never saw her again.

13

WE SHOULD ALL GO BROKE

When you only have $20.65 left to your name the rules change. Health doesn't matter anymore. Sports don't matter anymore. Technology doesn't matter anymore. All past choices don't matter one fucking bit. The weather doesn't matter. World problems don't matter. How that cup of coffee tastes doesn't matter. How old that apple is doesn't matter. What clothes you're wearing doesn't matter. How skinny you've gotten doesn't matter. The fact your glasses are crooked because you slept on them doesn't matter. Your barbecue being out of propane doesn't matter. Your left testicle aching more than normal doesn't matter. Dreaming of the good times doesn't matter.

Some things do matter, though. How you still treat others. How you care for the person suffering with you. How you buy into the depression that comes with being broke matters (i.e. you try with every power in your Being not to). How you love, how you laugh matter. How you enjoy the sunset matters. How you sit in awe of the Swallows gliding matters. A firm handshake matters. A smile matters. A joke matters. Enjoying the rising sun matters.

Why was I broke? A lot of reasons. Mainly because I had no Plan B. I just went with Plan A and got the shit kicked out of me until I was crying myself to sleep because I couldn't pay for groceries.

Being broke is bad. But it can end up being good.

14

YOU CAN'T BE IN LOVE WHEN YOU'RE A KID

She was the first girl people made fun of me for liking. I didn't like her, though. Well, I did, but I wasn't allowed to show it. It was too embarrassing. She wasn't an athlete or anything. I mean, we did go skiing with her family a couple times, and she was a far better skier than I was. But she dressed funny and wore glasses. Kind of like me. Let me rephrase that. I wore glasses, barely, because I would rather be blind then have them on my face, and I wore sweatpants to school everyday. I also wore wristbands (ie. sweatbands that ball players wear on their wrists or forearms) every day until high school. So I dressed funny too. But I was good at all sports at school and she didn't even play anything.

Some of the people I went to school with, years later, told me they saw us kissing once at recess. I don't remember that. I don't remember my first kiss. But the official story is that it happened during communion at church when the lips of a possessed young girl attacked me.

Every Valentine's Day from grade four until grade eight I would get a specially made card from her. She would get a standard card from me. The same one everybody else got.

We would walk the same direction home for ten minutes until she took a right and I continued straight. It was the same routine for nearly five years.

Once she defended me in front of the entire class as they laughed hysterically at me because I was caught on camera during the Christmas play vigorously picking my nose. I was an elf in the background. My dad was the man holding the video camera that caught this mess. She assured everyone I was simply scratching my nose while I was looking for the nearest window to jump out of.

Sometimes in the summer we would go for bike rides and talk. She was a brilliant girl. She could read entire novels in a day. I was an athlete so I didn't read. At thirteen, she wrote a novel and won a literary prize. Incredible, but I didn't get the whole writing a novel thing. It was for nerds. I wasn't a nerd. I was an athlete.

I liked her more in during the summer because it was only us. There were no kids around to make fun of me because she had a crush on me. I told them to leave me alone and that I didn't even like her.

The last time I remember seeing her was during the summer before high school. I might have seen her once since.

I don't know what she does now. Probably doing some fascinating work to save the world. She was always into that stuff.

Being a kid can suck. Even if you might like someone you can't act like you do because you'll get made fun of, and you don't want that so you just act like the feelings aren't mutual.

Those years between grade four and grade eight were some of the most popular years of my life. I didn't want to ruin that by saying I liked a girl who was a nerd. This coming from a guy who now writes books and barely does anything athletic anymore.

We went to different high schools and didn't see each other after that. I had taken my wristbands off and was wearing jeans now. I was different. I didn't think she would like the new me.

15

HOW TO BE A COWARD AND FIND HAPPINESS

I followed my then girlfriend to Virginia. I knew I couldn't work since I am Canadian. I could visit for six months and then come back to Canada and then go back to Virginia. I saved up over $12,000 to go and move there with her. I came back $8,000 in debt.

Why did I go? I was scared she'd find somebody else. I was scared to be alone. I clung out of fear. She wanted me to come and she truly believed we could make it work, so I went.

I remember knowing deep down I shouldn't go but I did anyways. I was suffering from depression and the belief I was losing another part of my life was too disastrous to deal with. That already happened to me with another girlfriend when I left for school so I knew it would happen again. They always find somebody else.

We found a fairly pricey apartment and I helped pay for everything.

She was going to school and couldn't have a job either so we both had zero income coming in (except her loans). It was a lose/lose situation if I'd ever seen one.

I became so broke and depressed I decided to make a baseball comeback. I did and left for a team in Canada that signed me.

We stayed together for another year. The only time I went back to visit her I sat in the fetal position on the office floor in the gym I was working at. I didn't want to go. I wanted a fresh start but I couldn't say no. I kept saying yes. So I became more depressed.

Eventually our relationship came to a point where she was going back home to visit and if I didn't fly there to see her we were done. I didn't want to go back. For a month I agonized whether I should say yes or no.

I ended up saying no and went into an even deeper depression. I didn't think I was depressed. I thought I was free. But I kept making weird choices to help fill a void in my life I thought I needed to be happy.

Then a miracle happened. I met my wife. Actually it was a miracle she kept persisting her pursuit of me. I seriously lack the skill of knowing when somebody is hitting on me.

I'm still fighting out of the debt I built by following and never standing my ground. I let fear exhaust me.

There's a popular saying in wrestling: Exhaustion makes cowards of us all.

That deals with all aspects of exhaustion: physical, emotional, mental, spiritual.

I was emotionally and mentally exhausted by fear and I cowered. And it cost me years of happiness.

But it helped me find the happiness I was always searching for.

And since I've found it how can I be angry at those years of always saying yes.

16

MY FINAL AND MOST MEANINGFUL SPEECH

It was my last major speech of the summer as head coach to the guys. Immediately after game one of the playoffs. My guys were tired and ready for a break. We had just been crushed 12-2.

There was a nice mix of rookies and veteran players on the squad. I could see the younger guys not feeling so hurt we were being dismantled. Not that they weren't trying, they were just ready for the end of the season, and, after what we'd been through as a team that summer, I couldn't blame them.

We signed "Luff" mid-season. I didn't want to sign him, but we needed him. To me, he was too unpredictable. It would be his last season playing at this college level because he would be ineligible next year. He wanted to finish wearing the Beavers jersey. After back and forth talks between myself and the general manager, we signed him.

Instantly some of the younger guys were hanging around him and it made me nervous. I couldn't get a read on what he was all about.

As our playoff push intensified so did he. I've never seen such an enthusiastic, "never say die" attitude from a player. With all of his heart he cared about the effort of the guys.

As we were getting our asses beat, it made me think of my final year playing. I knew it was my last. I was going to retire no matter what. I remembered how much I cared about everybody's effort during my final playoffs because it would be my last.

I saw the same thing in "Luff." Even down by ten he was urging the guys to keep pushing. But when you're young you believe your life in baseball is infinite, so it was hard for them to agree with his enthusiasm. There were friends, family, and girlfriends waiting for them back home. They missed that, and knew there would be more days at the ballpark for them. I was like that too when I first entered college.

So, as I gathered them in shallow left field for the post-game chat all I had were memories of my final game on replay in my head.

I began talking about results being what they were: results. I believed the effort was there so they had nothing to be ashamed of. Then I reminded them of the critical truth we all, at some point, hide from. This will not last forever. For some of the men dressed in uniform that night it would be their last season at that level.

The young guys didn't understand that yet, but, one day, it will be them playing their last game. And they will be fully invested in how the young guns are using their effort.

"Take a moment and think about the men you've fought with all summer. The one's maybe playing their final games. Respect them, respect the team, respect the game. Play your heart out for the one's who will never or already have seen their last days on the field. One day, it will be you."

It is a speech I'm proud I made. During the talk "Luff" was at full attention, nodding. He knew what I said was true.

We were swept out of the playoffs, but they showed true heart. I respected everything they did that summer. We went down as a team and that's all you can ever ask for.

A few days later the guys shipped out of town. I hopped in my car to get married.

One cold, rainy night in December of that year, before heading to a Christmas party, I was told some horrible news.

"Luff" was dead. He was killed in a horrific automobile accident during a snowstorm. I was shocked and saddened. It was the first time I ever lost a player I coached. I only knew him for about a month but I cared about him, as I did all my players.

I reflected back on the summer, his passion for the game, and making people smile. How, even when we are getting pummelled in life, we are lucky to get another day, to give it another go, and it should never be taken for granted. You need to play your heart out every day.

That summer "Luff" wore a baseball jersey for the last time. But, boy, did he wear it proudly.

No matter how you have failed in life or what you will fail at in the future, never stop playing. Don't stop having fun and never take yourself too seriously.

Be the best person you know how to be today. One day, it will be your last day. Take every failure as a lesson to help improve your life, or at least laugh at them.

It's good to laugh.

It's good to teach what you've learned.

It's good to dance unattached from fear.

It's good to share what you want to share.

It's good to live.

So live.

ABOUT THE AUTHOR

Daniel CJ Grant is a writer. He lives in Victoria, BC, with his wife and puppy. If you'd truly like to know more about what he does then it is highly recommended you venture to his website right now.

http://www.danielcjgrant.com